Heiner 11/99

Children
of the
TRAIL WEST

Children
of the
TRAIL WEST

Holly Littlefield

Carolrhoda Books, Inc./Minneapolis

Page one: Girls watch over the cooking on the Oregon Trail.
Page two: Stopping to rest on a log bridge
Opposite page: A Mormon wagon train takes a break from the trail.

The publisher wishes to thank Barbara Handy-Marchello, Associate Professor of History at the University of North Dakota, for her assistance in reviewing the manuscript.

Carolrhoda Books, Inc., c/o The Lerner Publishing Group
241 First Avenue North, Minneapolis, MN 55401 U.S.A.

Website address: www.lernerbooks.com

LIBRARY OF CONGRESS CATALOGING-IN-PUBLICATION DATA

Littlefield, Holly, 1963–
     Children of the trail west / Holly Littlefield.
        p.   cm. — (Picture the American past)
     Includes index.
     Summary: Explores the experiences of American children who traveled west to Oregon or California on wagon trains between 1841 and 1869, focusing on transportation, chores, recreation, and dangers.
      ISBN 1-57505-304-7
      1. Pioneer children—West (U.S.)—Social life and customs—Juvenile literature. 2. Frontier and pioneer life—West (U.S.)—Juvenile literature. 3. Overland journeys to the Pacific—Juvenile literature. 4. West (U.S.)—History—Juvenile literature.
     [1. Pioneers. 2. Overland journeys to the Pacific. 3. Frontier and pioneer life—West (U.S.) 4. West (U.S.)—History.] I. Title.
     II. Series.
     F593.L58 1999
     978'.02—dc21   98-3153

Manufactured in the United States of America
1 2 3 4 5 6 – JR – 04 03 02 01 00 99

CONTENTS

During the 1800s, thousands of families like this one went west in search of a better life.

Jumping Off

Eastward I go only by force; but Westward I go free. . . .
I must walk toward Oregon.
— Henry David Thoreau, 1862

Wagons ho! Between 1841 and 1869, nearly half a million Americans traveled west on wagon trains. These travelers called themselves emigrants because they were leaving the United States to go to the territories of Oregon, California, or Utah.

People went west for many reasons. Some wanted gold, adventure, or a warmer climate. Many came to claim land for farms. Others, such as the Mormons, wanted a place to practice their religion in peace.

These African Americans traveled to Kansas in the 1870s, but others went as far west as California or Oregon.

Thousands of African Americans went west. Some were forced to go as the slaves of white emigrants. Others traveled west to find land, jobs, or gold. By 1860, about 5,500 African Americans lived in the western territories.

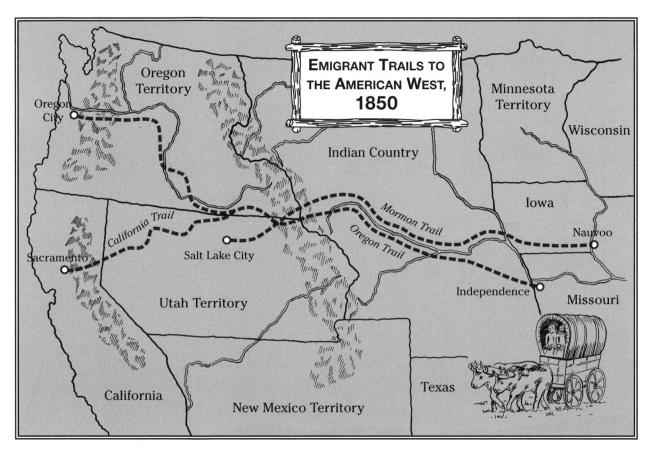

There were several trails west, but none was easy. Most families took the northern routes called the Oregon, California, and Mormon Trails.

The journey would take more than six months and cover over two thousand miles. To help plan the trip, people used guidebooks that other travelers had written. These books had maps and advice, but sometimes they gave bad directions, too.

Towns like Lawrence, Kansas, grew into popular jumping-off places.

Most families sold almost everything they owned before leaving. Children parted with toys, books, and extra clothes. The wagon would have room only for supplies.

Next, families journeyed to a jumping-off place. This was a town near the start of the trails. Here, the emigrants bought supplies and built wagons. They also joined a wagon train and elected a leader. Boys as young as 14 voted in these elections. Girls didn't get a vote.

An emigrant wagon had to be strong. Its base was carefully sealed with tar to make it waterproof. The wagon would have to serve as a boat for crossing rivers.

The top of the wagon was covered with heavy white fabric, stretched across wooden hoops called bows. Girls helped their mothers sew the fabric and coat it with oil to keep out the rain.

This wagon's cover has been pulled up to show the bows.

Oxen were stronger than horses but not as stubborn as mules. These oxen were part of a wagon train festival in 1906.

Most emigrants chose oxen to pull their wagons. Oxen were strong and would eat grass on the trail. The family would not have to carry feed for them. Children had to be careful not to get crushed under the oxen's heavy feet.

This re-creation of an emigrant wagon is crammed with a spinning wheel, silverware, a butter churn, and a kerosene lamp.

Everything the family needed had to fit in the wagon. Children could bring only small things—maybe a doll, a diary, or a pocketknife. Clothes, quilts, and barrels of food filled the inside of the wagon. Tools were hung outside.

Some Mormon families could not afford wagons, so they built pushcarts. Families pushed these two-wheeled carts 1,400 miles, from Illinois to Utah. Even young children helped push the carts up mountain trails and across rivers.

Pushcarts could be bigger than the children who pushed them.

Children hang onto their seats as their wagon train hits the trail.

Time to jump off! Most wagon trains began the journey in April or May. If they left too early, they would not find enough grass to feed their animals. If they left too late, they might get caught in mountain snowstorms.

Many children were excited to leave. Still, saying good-bye was hard. The children might never again see the friends and relatives they left behind. And what if they ran out of food or got lost on the trail?

Wagon wheels left deep ruts on the plains, making a trail for families like this one to follow.

On the Way West

You never know what will happen next, nor where you'll be tomorrow, when you are traveling in a covered wagon.
——Laura Ingalls Wilder,
Little House on the Prairie

The easiest part of the journey, crossing the Great Plains, came first. To the emigrants, the flat plains seemed to stretch on forever. Prairie grasses grew so tall that children could get lost in them.

Very small children might ride in the wagon or on a horse or mule, but most children walked, just as their parents and animals did.

Few emigrants rode in the wagons. They didn't want to add extra weight to the load. Most walked all day long, 10 to 20 miles each day. One boy remembered how his mother's feet swelled terribly from walking. She had to wrap them in cloth to keep them from bleeding.

Children of all ages worked hard on the wagon train. One important job was caring for the animals. Children milked cows and drove them along the trail. They gathered wood and buffalo droppings for fuel, too.

A woman and boy use whips to keep the oxen moving.

Children also helped find and prepare food for every meal. Boys carried guns and hunted. Children gathered berries as they walked. When hunting was bad or berries were scarce, meals were just beans, bread, and dried meat. Everyone, even children, drank coffee.

This boy and his sister are old enough to provide meals of berries and squirrel meat for their family.

Even at lunchtime, animals had to be unhitched and water had to be fetched.

Life on a wagon train followed a pattern. Everyone got up early. Children watered oxen, started pancakes, and packed wagons. By seven o'clock, they hit the trail. Nooning—a quick stop for lunch—was a welcome break for tired feet. But after a short rest and a cold meal, the emigrants traveled on until it was time to camp for the night.

A tent might not be as fun as the open air for sleeping, but it did a better job of keeping out bugs and snakes.

In camp, the wagons were parked in a circle for safety. Most families set up tents. Some children slept under the wagons, while others bedded down in the open air under the stars.

A fiddler entertains weary travelers in camp.

Although life in a wagon train was very hard, the emigrants tried to have fun. At night, they sang and danced to fiddle music. Children told stories, wrote letters, and played games. To celebrate the Fourth of July or a wedding, mothers might make lemonade or gingerbread.

The emigrants buried in these graves died in 1844 and 1845.

Trouble on the Trail

They swum the deep rivers and clumb the high peaks,
They rolled thro' the country for many long weeks,
Thro' all sorts of misery, dry days and wet,
If they hadn't gone on, they'd be campin' there yet.
—from "Sweet Betsey from Pike,"
a folk song written in 1858

About one out of every ten emigrants, including many children, died on the trail west. Some were crushed by wagon wheels or drowned while crossing rivers. Most were killed by illnesses like cholera. Every few miles, the wagon trains passed another trailside grave.

Water is too scarce for these dust-covered emigrants to take baths. Every drop is needed for drinking.

The weather also caused problems. Sudden, terrible rainstorms left the emigrants surrounded by mud. At other times, the weather was very dry. The wagons stirred up clouds of dust that hung in the air like fog. Dirt covered everything, even the emigrants' food.

Horses strain to pull a wagon across a river.

Emigrants faced many dangerous river crossings. The animals had to wade or swim across, pulling the wagons behind them. During one crossing, a girl and her two-year-old sister were swept a mile downstream in their wagon. The quick-thinking girl grabbed the wagon bows and held her sister's head above the water, saving them both.

Many children were afraid of meeting Indians along the trail. However, few Indians harmed the travelers. Many helped with directions and river crossings.

As more wagon trains traveled west, some Indians became less friendly. The emigrants brought new diseases. They also killed the buffalo that the Indians needed for food and shelter. And they demanded more and more land. These conflicts grew into wars that drove the native peoples from their homes.

A family of Blackfeet Indians. The Blackfeet once lived on the Great Plains, but lost their homes to white emigrants.

Emigrants pull a wagon piece by piece up a rocky cliff. Harold Von Schmidt painted this picture many years after the last wagon train went west.

Crossing the mountains was one of the hardest parts of the journey. Some trails were so steep that the emigrants had to pull their wagons up with ropes.

Going down was often just as hard. Wagons could break apart or race out of control. Sometimes wagon trains traveled less than a mile a day.

Many wagons were too heavy. The oxen couldn't pull the loads over the rough, steep trails. The travelers had to leave behind furniture, stoves, tools, and clothes. Even a doll or a book might be too heavy to keep.

A rickety railing makes this mountain trail safer for tired animals.

Every emigrant feared winter in the mountains. Early snowstorms blocked trails and left wagon trains stranded. Even families who planned well sometimes ran out of food. Many travelers ate their oxen to survive. Some even ate their shoes!

This family has two hardy mules, a camp stove, and a pile of quilts to help them get through the Rocky Mountains.

An artist's image of members of the Donner Party, their wagons left behind, struggling up a snowy mountainside in the Sierra Nevada

A wagon train called the Donner party was trapped for months in the mountains by heavy winter snows. Thirteen-year-old Virginia Reed described her terrible ordeal. "We had to kill little Cash the dog and eat him," she wrote.

When their food and animals ran out, some of the travelers had to eat the bodies of people who had already died. Only 41 of the 83 snowbound emigrants survived.

Trails through the desert were bumpy, dusty, and dry as bones.

After the mountains, many emigrants had to cross hot deserts. Children covered their lips and faces with black axle grease to keep them from burning and cracking in the sun. Some families walked for days with almost nothing to drink. Only the hope of finding water kept them going.

A wagon train arrives in Helena, in the territory of Montana, in the 1870s.
Can you spot the telegraph poles on the town's main street?

A New Home

[California] is a beautiful Country. . . .
It ought to be a beautiful Country to pay us
for our trouble getting there.
—Virginia Reed, age 13, 1847

At last, the journey ended. Often, people from a wagon train settled together in small towns or in cities like San Francisco or Portland.

The emigrants still faced hardships. Many lived in their wagons for months until they could afford to build houses.

Hardworking miners use a fast stream of water to search rocky soil for gold in California.

Some emigrants settled in mining towns. During the 1840s and 1850s, people rushed to California to look for gold. Many came from as far away as China. Children worked beside their fathers, panning and digging for gold nuggets and dust. But very few people found much. Most took other jobs or returned home, disappointed.

These boys are lucky to have this sturdy log cabin as their home.

Some families built log cabins in the country, miles from the nearest neighbor. These one-room houses had dirt floors and few windows. Later, when the settlers could afford it, they built larger houses from boards instead of logs.

Many emigrants became farmers. They started their farms with only the tools and seeds they had brought west. Children worked alongside their parents, just as they had on the trail. When they grew up, many started farms and families of their own.

A woman plows soil outside a tiny farmhouse in what would become Idaho.

For years, people who went west by train still needed wagons to pick them up where the tracks ended.

The trip west changed in 1869. The country was linked from coast to coast by the Transcontinental Railroad. Families with enough money could travel west by train. Soon the days of the huge wagon trains ended. But the children who journeyed west in covered wagons never forgot the hardships and excitement of the trail.

TRAIL TREATS
A Recipe for Gingerbread

Spit in my ears and tell me lies,
But give me no dried apple pies.
　　　　　—words to an emigrant folk song

Kids didn't get to have treats very often on the trail west. Sugar was expensive and had to last all the way west. Dried apples were the only fruit that wouldn't spoil on the trip. So the emigrants ate dried apple pie or berries for dessert—when they were lucky.

One day was different, though. On the Fourth of July, almost every wagon train took a break from the trail. The emigrants celebrated the holiday with picnics, parades, speeches, and songs. Women and girls sewed American flags and hung them from the wagons. Men and boys hunted game for a feast.

And feast they did. They ate baked beans, potatoes, and rabbit stew. Girls and women made lemonade—not with lemons, but with drops of lemon extract. They made cakes, pies, and gingerbread, too. The emigrants usually didn't have chickens to lay eggs for their cakes. So they did without. The cakes still tasted wonderful.

Emigrants baked their treats in a skillet over an open fire, or beside the fire on a heated rock or the blade of a hoe. In this recipe, you will bake gingerbread in an oven. The emigrants didn't have all the ingredients you will use. They had no vegetable oil spray, white sugar, or modern baking soda. But this gingerbread will taste a lot like a Fourth of July treat on the trail west.

GINGERBREAD

1/2 cup butter*
vegetable oil spray
1/2 cup sugar
1/2 cup molasses
2 cups flour
1 tablespoon ginger
1/2 teaspoon baking soda
1/4 teaspoon salt
1/2 cup water

1. Preheat oven to 350 degrees Fahrenheit. Set butter out to soften (or soften in a microwave oven by heating on medium for 15 seconds).

*Many emigrants brought cows with them so they could have fresh milk and butter on the trail. When butter wasn't available, cooks used bacon fat or other meat drippings.

2. Use vegetable oil spray to grease the bottom and sides of an 8-inch cake pan or a 9-inch pie pan. Add about a teaspoon of flour. Tilt the pan so that flour covers bottom and sides.

3. When butter is soft, mix with sugar and molasses in a large bowl. Stir well to get rid of lumps.

4. In a medium-sized bowl, mix flour, ginger, baking soda, and salt. Stir about half of the flour mixture into the butter mixture. Mix until blended. Batter will be very thick.

5. Pour water into a kettle. Warm on stovetop at high heat until the water boils. Ask an adult to measure the water and pour about half over the batter. Stir until batter is runny and has no lumps.

6. Stir the rest of the flour mixture into batter and mix well. Ask an adult to add the rest of the hot water. Mix until completely blended, with no lumps. Batter will be thick but still runny.

7. Pour batter into pan. Spread evenly with a spatula. Ask an adult to put pan in the oven, using an oven mitt. Bake for 40 to 45 minutes. The adult can test the gingerbread by inserting a toothpick into the center. When toothpick comes out clean, gingerbread is ready. Let cool about 30 minutes before cutting.

Makes 8 large or 16 small slices. To store, cover with aluminum foil.

NOTE TO TEACHERS AND ADULTS

For children, the days of the wagon trains may seem like part of a distant and far-off past. But there are many ways to make the trail west and its people come alive. Along with helping children cook up trail treats like gingerbread, you can explore America's westward expansion in other ways. One way is to read more about the trail west. More books on the topic are listed on pages 45 and 46. Another way to explore the past is to train young readers to study historical photographs. Historical photographs hold many clues about how life was lived in earlier times.

Ask your children or students to look for the details and "read" all the information in each picture in this book. For example, how is the street on page 10 different from a typical modern street? (Before the automobile was invented, many streets were built wide. Since wagons and carts were pulled by harnessed animals, they needed plenty of room to turn around.) Why are stones piled on top of the graves on page 24? (Emigrants didn't have time to dig deep graves when someone died on the trail. Sometimes they had no wood for coffins, either. So they piled stones on graves to keep animals from digging up the bodies. The stones also served as a marker.)

To teach young readers to read historical photographs, have them try these activities:

Packing for the Journey West

Study the photo of a well-packed wagon on page 13. What supplies and other goods can you see in the photograph? Based on what you can see and what you have read, write a list of all the things a young settler would need on the trip west in the 1800s. Next, imagine that you are moving to a new place. Write a list of the things you would take with you. Compare your lists. How do you think travel and life have changed over the years? How would your list change if you could take only what would fit in a covered wagon?

Keeping a Journal

Many emigrants, both adults and children, kept written records of their journey west. Sometimes the emigrants sent these journals back home for friends or relatives to read. Imagine yourself as a young member of a wagon train. Write a journal to send to the best friend you've left behind at home. Describe each part of your trip as though it has just happened. Did your wagon get stuck in mud on the plains? How did you react to meeting Indians? Did you make it through the mountains before winter snows started? What kind of home did your family find in the West? Include entries about the chores you did and the dangers you faced.

Kids on the Trail

Dress up in costume and tell your friends, parents, or classmates what it was like to be a child on the trail west. Read the text—and the photos—in this book for information and for details about daily life. To add to your presentation, read some of the books on pages 45 and 46. You could act out the part of Hattie from *Across the Wide and Lonesome Prairie*, Jesse from *A Fourth of July on the Plains*, or Ginny from *Wagon Train*. Or read *I Walked to Zion* and tell the story of a young Mormon emigrant's journey to Utah.

Resources on the Trail West

Duncan, Dayton. *The West: An Illustrated History for Children.* New York: Little, Brown and Company, 1996. One of three companion books for children to the PBS television series *The West*, this volume combines historical photographs with the stories of the people of the American West.

Gregory, Kristiana. *Across the Wide and Lonesome Prairie: The Oregon Trail Diary of Hattie Campbell, 1847.* New York: Scholastic Inc., 1997. This novel takes the form of a diary kept by thirteen-year old Hattie Campbell as her family travels west on the Oregon Trail.

Madsen, Susan Arington. *I Walked to Zion: True Stories of Young Pioneers on the Mormon Trail.* Salt Lake City, Utah: Deseret Book Company, 1994. In their own words, emigrants who traveled the Mormon Trail as children tell how they pushed carts to Utah in search of religious freedom.

Miller, Brandon Marie. *Buffalo Gals: Women of the Old West.* Minneapolis, Minn.: Lerner Publications Company, 1995. Using excerpts from diaries, letters, and travel guides, Miller paints a picture of the lives of girls and women on the western frontier.

Sandler, Martin W. *Pioneers: A Library of Congress Book.* New York: HarperCollins Publishers, 1994. Sandler uses photographs from the Library of Congress to bring to life the Americans who went west, the Indians who lost their homes, and the cities and railroads that grew as a result.

Stefoff, Rebecca. *Children of the Westward Trail.* Brookfield, Conn.: Millbrook Press, 1996. This book for middle readers describes the daily life of emigrant children, the dangers of their journey, and the new homes they found in the West.

Stein, R. Conrad. *The Oregon Trail.* Chicago: Children's Press, 1994. Illustrated with historical photographs and prints, this volume discusses the history of the Oregon Trail from the arrival of the first white explorers to the emigration and settlement of thousands of Americans.

Van Leeuwen, Jean. Illustrated by Henri Sorensen. *A Fourth of July on the Plains.* New York: Dial Books for Young Readers, 1997. In a story based on a real celebration on the Oregon Trail in 1852, everyone plans to contribute to the wagon train's Fourth of July party—except Jesse, who's too young to do much of anything. Then he thinks of a clever way to make his own mark on the festivities.

Wright, Courtni C. Illustrated by Gershom Griffith. *Wagon Train: A Family Goes West in 1865.* New York: Holiday House, 1995. This fictional account tells the story of Ginny, a former slave whose family faces snakebite, thirst, and dust as they journey to California after the Civil War.

Website   http://www.isu.edu/~trinmich/Oregontrail.html
Part of PBS Online, this Website from the creators of the documentary film *The Oregon Trail* features "Fantastic Facts" about the westward journey, quotes from emigrants and historians, and historic sites to visit.

New Words

bows: wooden hoops on a covered wagon. Fabric was stretched across the bows to make a cover that would keep out rain and dust.

cholera: a disease, spread by dirty food and water, that can cause death

emigrant: a person who leaves one country to move to another. Americans who went west in the mid-1800s called themselves emigrants because they were going to places that were not yet, or had only recently become, part of the United States.

jumping-off place: a town near the beginning of the trails west. Families bought supplies, built wagons, and joined wagon trains in jumping-off places.

nooning: stopping for lunch and rest on the trail west

pushcart: a two-wheeled cart that was pushed by hand. Many Mormon families used pushcarts because they cost less than wagons did.

Transcontinental Railroad: a railroad that joined the East and West Coasts of the United States in 1869

Index

TIME LINE

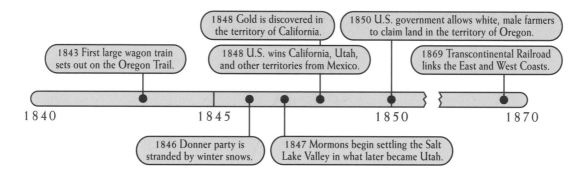

1848 Gold is discovered in the territory of California.

1850 U.S. government allows white, male farmers to claim land in the territory of Oregon.

1843 First large wagon train sets out on the Oregon Trail.

1848 U.S. wins California, Utah, and other territories from Mexico.

1869 Transcontinental Railroad links the East and West Coasts.

1840   1845   1850   1870

1846 Donner party is stranded by winter snows.

1847 Mormons begin settling the Salt Lake Valley in what later became Utah.

ABOUT THE AUTHOR

Holly Littlefield has been a columnist, a waitress, a manuscript reader, a high school English teacher, and a volunteer counselor for runaway teens. She is pursuing a Ph.D. in English. She lives in Minneapolis with her husband, two sons, and golden retriever. This is her fourth book for children.

"Every time I cross the Rocky Mountains," she says, "I am amazed and inspired by the courage and determination of the emigrants who crossed those mountains in wagons. It must have taken amazing bravery to set out with your family and a few supplies on a six-month journey across the wilderness. I'm not sure that many of us today would manage to survive the trip!"

PHOTO ACKNOWLEDGMENTS

The photographs in this book are reproduced through the courtesy of: Kansas State Historical Society, Topeka, Kansas, front cover, pp. 10, 17 (detail), 20, 27; Ben Wittick, courtesy Museum of New Mexico, Neg. No. 3083, back cover (detail), p. 21; Oregon Historical Society, pp. 1 (#OrHi 5237-A) (detail), 37 (#OrHi 36118); Denver Public Library, Western History Department, pp. 2, 6, 18, 25 (detail), 26, 30, 33; Mormon emigrants at Coalville, Utah, ca. 1867 © LDS Church Archives, p. 5; [Man, woman, and child in front of covered wagon] Amon Carter Museum, Fort Worth, Texas, pp. 7 (detail), 11; Library of Congress, pp. 8, 12, 19; Lejla Fazlic Omerovic, pp. 9, 41; National Archives, p. 13; Archive Photos, pp. 14, 39; Courtesy of the Nebraska State Historical Society, Solomon D. Butcher Collection, RG2068-2983A, p. 16; Colorado Historical Society, #20280, p. 22; North Wind Picture Archives, p. 23; Wyoming State Museum, p. 24; Smithsonian Institution National Anthropological Archives, Bureau of American Ethnology Collection, Neg. No. 430-C-3, p. 28; Baldwin H. Ward/Corbis-Bettmann, p. 29; Colorado Springs Pioneers Museum, Starsmore Center for Local History, p. 31; California History Section, California State Library, p. 32; Montana Historical Society, Helena, p. 34; Peter E. Palmquist, pp. 35 (detail), 36; Idaho State Historical Society, #3201, p. 38.

12/99